Where Everything Lost is Found

Alejandra Reuhel

ISBN-13: 978-0989931403

ISBN-10: 0989931404

© Sub Verse Publishing
  Puerto Rico

sub
VERSE

This book is for everyone who has ever felt lost in a familiar place.

A.R.

Contents

Where Everything
Lost is Found

Ribbon

I never thought I'd see the sky spiraling
down into a blue strip of silken ribbon,
landing soft and silent on my open hands.

It floated quietly, quietly, down, as space
became a vacuum. The ground remained
under my feet, but the overwhelming
emptiness forced me to my knees, the
weight of the void pressing down upon me.

I gently smoothed the ribbon with my
fingers, out into a linear strip, and it
stretched, all by itself, twitching, writhing
like a dying insect.

I burst into tears because I didn't know
what was wrong, or even if there was
anything wrong at all...

The sky had transformed and fallen, and
now it lay on the ground like an electrified
serpent.

My tears fell, hot and heavy, on its surface, and it liquefied, starting at the wet dots of tear stains.

Little by little, it became a thin river… it turned from blue to black, and, within the fluid, there were tiny spots of white lights… the night sky became a river!
I was afraid to look up, afraid of what I might see above, so I looked down, down into the night river.

I leaned in close to the stream of sky and it didn't seem as much like a river anymore.

I closed my eyes and listened to the distant melody that seemed to emanate from the space-fluid, and, at the same time, from a memory I was unsure was even mine.

I was seduced by sleep and fell into the sky.

I could have drowned. I knew.

It didn't matter.

I. In Gardens

Star

I found the sky underwater
Airless, where I could not breathe
The suffocating blue, so clear
Through muffled, slow heart beats

THUMP (I think I'll drown here)
THUMP (I think I'll freeze)
THUMP (I think I've found my place)
THUMP (I have indeed)

Coat

She used to wear
a velvet coat
that everyone would notice
since
it had so many colors that
it gave her new found
innocence
But

                                    she,
                    she does not wear
                               it now,
                        she fell into
                          a puddle

of ink, I think
she knew she'd slip
(It's easier to stumble.)

                  She likes ink rain,
                she's loved the pain
                    of broken ankles
                  and stars that sing

But velvet coats
of colors
and colors, they

Never
served
of use for anything

        She used to wear
         a velvet coat
        but now she only
         wears her skin

            that has no color, you see
               when she fell,
        she was covered in blackest ink

She cries sometimes,
she thinks she's lost
a never-had purity
 Yet pure as black

             and white she lacks
              a sense of reality

She wears a cloak
of misery

that everyone does gaze upon

She wears her spirit's nudity
and seldom feels that this is wrong

Wish

Instead of wishing for useful things
I wished hard for a pair of feathered wings

Instead I was granted a lovely song
To remind me of something I could have
done wrong

Done it twice, three times or four
But isn't it enough to always want more?

Now I think I should have gone
And done what I would have, and done it
all wrong

Because I can always wish for pairs of
wings
And not have them granted, but have better
things

I'm young and I'm ignorant, that's what I
use
To justify wishes, my age, an excuse

I act like I'm old as I try to act young
Like a child who doesn't know how to have
fun

A little girl dressed as a doll-like bad dream
Nursing nightmares and cobwebs, year-
round Halloween

If only a had a huge pair of wings
I'd be happy and not so concerned for these
things.

Fish

Fading in a fishtank sky
Fading into blue
You've faded, please excuse that I
Keep all these memories of you

Excuse me, wait, excuse my words,
That isn't what I meant…
I meant that I had
remembered it wrong,
I confused it with something
That I must have dreamt…

The dream was about you and the midday
sky,
Silence and starless sleep
I sleep too much sometimes, you know,
To get lost and find secrets that aren't mine
to keep

Fade with me, underwater,
Won't you? Fade into my fishtank sky
Where you shall remain forever

With a song and a wish (and a fish) and a
sigh.

A sigh into a fishtank basement
Faded beauty, loved
Drowned below the starless weight
Of skies that shift forever above

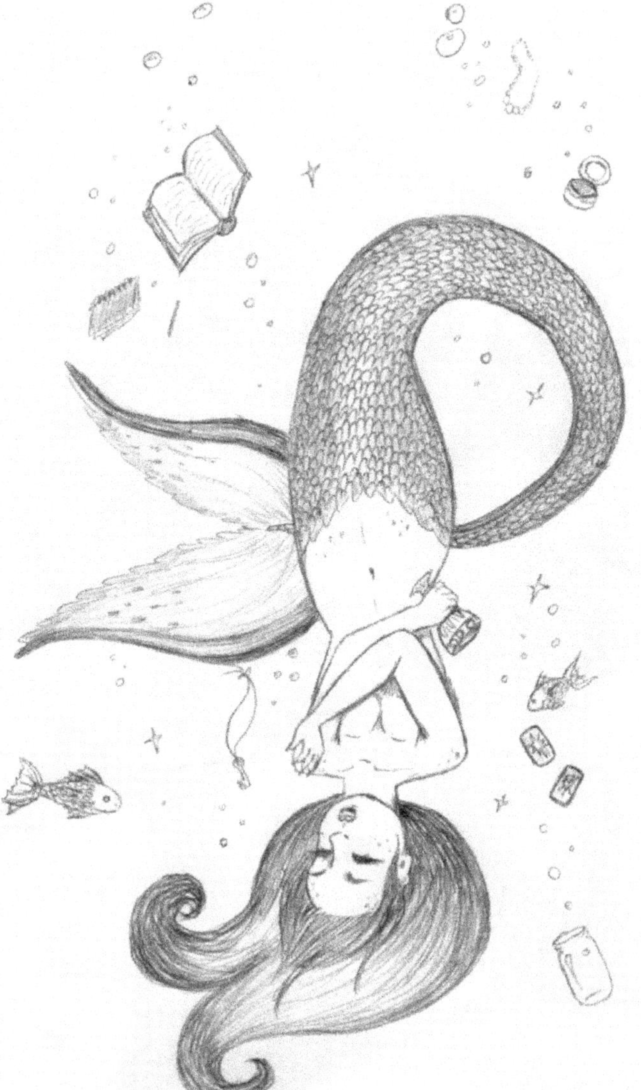

Serpents

I tried to let
A moment in
But serpents crawl
Under my skin

My eyelids on
The insides have
A sky enamored
With the past

An insect lives
Inside my ears
That screams into
My mind my fears

Under my nails
Sometimes grow
Sharp, thin razors
Hid below

The sleeves of my
Guilt-stricken soul
I wear as a
Pure, clean white robe

Tangled in
Between my hair
Cling thoughts that grew eyes,
Now they stare

At me, they find
A way inside
So they can mutate
In my mind

And turn to monsters,
Coming back
To scare me
(Yes, I'm scared by that!)

Insects

I'll let the insects crawl about
My skin, and let them eat away
The sugar and the salt, the sweet -
But only for today they prey

Spiders, they shall creep inside
To hollow out my head
As worms make way,
They crawl out through my eyes
and there, build sparkling webs

I could shake them off, I could
Stand to my feet, up from the ground
But for now, I'll be carrion,
I'll feed them all,
In my bones, they're safe and sound

They can eat away my skin, and slowly
Come inside, in through my ears
Leave me with no tongue, no eyes
No heart, no flesh, no nerves to feel.

It had an angel to every corner of heaven flooding over me, a saint each one. he was, each in his own twisted, martyrized way. My angels, know I love you still and always will.

A feather falls with every moment condemned to oblivion, and so it is that, year upon year, these wings will become flightless. And that is my unoriginal offer to you, where my heart will not do, where words don't and cannot.

tale is just as good as blood, a bird shot down by cruel stones from an innocent's hand. The hands of love, breathes in their breathing over a mind that flies higher than the seraphs as they took their holy flights over the living... dreams die where memories live.

Mother

I fell dreaming
Of the fragrance
Of roses and jasmines
Saw a lady
    -   a beauty
just quietly standing

Are you my mother?

My loneliness poisons me

You are my mother
Beloved Destiny

Petals and droplets
Of thinned blood and sweet dew
Will always remain
Bright red, as they do

I dream of pain in metaphors
Here, they transform into roses
I wish for the tame and tranquil breezes,
The swish-swishing waves of the ocean

Lady in white
My spinner of Life
Forgive me when I curse your name
I come to cry dewdrop tears on your
shoulder,
Red drops on your Jasmine dress, stained.

There's a place, far away,
Where the sky meets the sea
You'll take me there, Mother,
You promised me.

As a child I am wretched,
But still, I am small
And you, lady of Jasmines,
Stand before me, so tall

I can't stop these red tears…

I've made such a mess…

I've gone and I've ruined
Your lovely white dress

You're so beautiful, still
I just wish to stop crying
Red petals coat
The floor, dead and drying

Perfumed of Destiny's
Mother of dreams
Jasmines and roses
And the warm ocean's breeze

Curled at your feet

I will sleep,
I will sleep

Graylands

Serpentine vines
Crawl up and slither
Up 'round my spine
Where their pink blossoms whither

Petrified eyes
Cry crystal dew drops
Deep sorrowed sighs
In the form of white frost

Vicious green roots
Like spider legs cling
To the soles of my boots
Paralyzing

Rupturing skin,
Crept their way to my bones
Found their way in
Wrung me dry as a stone

Forcing my gaze
Toward a vast field of Spring
While I stand in the haze,
Eden's gay, flourishing

Shriveling black buds
Tangled dry in my hair
Is the land's poisoned blood,
Flowers with deathly airs

Floral death I inhale,
As I watch paradise
I can only exhale
Smoke with fragments of ice

The faithless, condemned
To the graylands, cold nothing
With a cold heart, defend
That I once stood for something

I stand now, but frozen,
Where angels don't sing
All dusty, dead, broken
In a field of black Spring

Garden

The water is purple
And scented of Jasmines
The day has four New Moons
Kneel by the river and help me catch fish
In my shiny, glass balloon.

Then fasten a chain to my waist (as I float),
Pull me strongly to your side -
I shall pull out the stars from my fingernails
To become the black starred sky's bride.

After I free it, the snake in my mouth,
With its tail curling 'round my weak spine.
(It makes me hiss and makes me say
Words that are really not mine.)

Watercolors drip freely, as it slips,
In a spiral, spinning, swirling, twirling
down.
A chair of red velvet from the tapestry room
Is being swallowed by the forest's humid
ground.

Decompose, like leaves,
Flowers blossom from stale death,
I always pray my muses to inspire
So purple rivers flow
And turquoise jasmines grow
So this perfumed dream of gardens won't
expire.

Nightsong

Selene shone half of her beautiful face
With nine points all around her
As I, cold and insignificant lay
Trying hard not to whimper any louder

With a heavy hand extended
Weaving circles in the air
And one upon my heart, intending
To invite the other there

But there were too many sounds
Too much artificial light
And too many lies I believe in
Too many noises polluting the night

Except the small, white fragrant flowers
That with the dawn, die on the ground
As I should flourish fast and whither
Or else in these fat childish tears I will
drown

Request

In a garden, like Eden, with blurred
memory's light,
As I sit under this tree
The midday sky grows silent
My darling boy siren, sing for me…

I don't have many words to say,
But many smiles for you
(As you don't have to say a word,
Just give me strips of blue).

And sing for me, my siren,
If you love me, kill me here.
Everything is beautiful,
But I'm haunted and haunted by fears.

I shall be yours, I want to be,
If you keep this memory…
Kill me as I know you will,
Keep on singing for me.

What lovely eyes have you, and your voice,
I am in love with you.
But love is like a moment, I know,
It will last only one or two.

My handsome siren, sing for me,
And kill me, if you will.
Make it last forever,
Grant this favor to the ill.

This tree will live longer than you, than I,
I'm fading, as a ghost.
From all the dreams I've had and lived,
I like this one the most.

Before night falls, claim me, siren,
Dead I shall be yours.
The day is beautiful (not more than you),
But I want to see no more.

Untitled

The day is bright (too bright)
But after dusk, then, finally
There's one moment of peace: a pen
And attempts at poetry

She bears her light of blue and white
Beneath her, still, I stand
Swooning below an immaculate sky,
A notebook in my hands

That I can only try to write, this sight,
Several meager words are scratched
Across the lines... They read, they say:
"The Moon is white. The sky is black."

There is no comfort yet, no means,
To mirror a reality
That bounces off into the ether,
Only poetry

Untitled

I had a thought,
Inappropriate (somewhat)
That I think I should not say.

But what do you do
When these thoughts come to you
And stay throughout the day?

II. House

There's a room

(from the inside)

that nobody knows

From the outside

 (the one

that has no windows)

Doors

Doors close behind me, not too far behind
Tapping me softly on my way out
While others start opening, in the same line
On the horizon, they opened there, and
near, all about…

Yet I choose to ride, as I always do,
On the passenger's side, looking out the
window
Or buried deep in narcoleptic half-sleep,
Floating down between lines in a book,
between scribbles
Such a strange girl

I am tired, always tired, *who am I?*
Just someone who finds stars in everyone's
eyes
Mining for what he might have, and what's
he got?
Songs a plenty from his hands and lips, a
luscious heart.

All doors seem to shut, closing at once,
Except for one (the smallest one)
To which I crawled and crept right through
Because I could, just because I thought:
There may be something for me here

I heard a song
I had learned ages ago
And remembered all along.

Like gusts of wind from seas to shore,
Like drafts from cracks between the doors,
Were feather by feather, by traces of dust,
Lifted and blown
Out to places unknown
Along with whatever we knew about us

Heart

I know there's a heart
At the end of a hall
Like a dream, like an unclear dead thought.
It's colored dark gray,
Or black, anyway,
There's a painting there, of a pink heart.

I know that it's beating,
Now dry, but once beating,
It just hangs in the pale, yellow light.
The room, cold as freezing,
The heart, thumping, beating,
In the silence of hallways at night.

The canvas, black steel,
It's almost unreal
As it's thumping the silence away
In a thorny wood frame
With a plaque with my name,
This gallery must be far away.

Not a thing I recall,
(If I've been there at all)
But the cold and the light, and the heart on
the wall.
In my eyelids it must be, painted inside,
For every time that I close my eyes,
Again, there I stand in the cold of the hall.

The Tapestry Room

This room has grown so weary of your
woes
The spiders have all hidden in their holes
Words no longer dance upon the air
for you to catch
And the walls no longer whisper songs to
hold

The sky shines bright outside, but tired, too
The stars, like dusty headlights, far away
No longer sing or sparkle, they will never
Wait for you
again, because you've asked them to please
stay

Inside a room than doesn't want you
like it used to
Its spaces and its graces are abused
As love can leave a heart so's left your spirit
from this place
Your sparks and flames and flutters've been
consumed

Locks

You have many secret rooms, confined
To which you have lost every key
I wonder what wonderful things there you
hide,
If they're full of unreal memories

Since you live in a hallway where haunts
decorate
Your walls and your carpet, the ceiling and
floor
Perhaps they are fond of and contemplate
That you sit in serenity against each closed
door

But who are these ghosts made of cobwebs
and dust?
They appear to be tranquil and sleeping
Perhaps they all know that your locks full of
rust
Should be opened, to stop you from
weeping

I wish I could see what you keep in those rooms,
Something special, I see, by the look in your eyes
By your motions and pallor, your silence and gloom,
There must be lovely monsters inside

But for now, I will leave, as I see that you grieve
In the loveliest of ways
Silence is beauty, (is what I believe)
I will question your secrets on some other day

Velvet Hall

You stood between a velvet wall
And a coffin, Onyx black
With gray pale skin and crystal eyes
Wings hanging from your back

"Am I about to die?" I asked
"Or about to fall asleep?"
You closed your crystal eyes and turned
So that I would not see you weep

And I was but a figure, blackened
Stranded in a forest of sounds
Electronic predatorial cries
Scaring and wearing me down

So I quickly glanced up at the moon
The only familiar celestial thing
I knew that you would not look at me
But I knew that her blue would be
shimmering

And for once, I did not want to see her
I would rather have been in your velvet hall

Where the ceiling was made of wires and
rust
My sky did not please me at all
I tried to walk to your coffin, to you
But I found I could not even breathe
Piercing vines had tied me down
And covered my body in leaves

Arachnids came and ate away
The verdure of my flesh
Florae then for a moment I'd been
Now a putrefactive mess

Of bones and roots, but upward remained
The image that never would lie
My Father, my hope, my forever, my Love
The blue black starred sky

I forgot about halls and your velvet walls,
Crying angels with crystalliferous eyes
And remembered, in wondrous consistency
Is where the remotest of comfort lies

I became as the Earth, and I only had sight
For my planets and guardian stars
For the moon that moved her way East to
the West

And the void that took up all forever's afar

Until Dawn touched me with violet
Forced I was to taste the faded hue
Of morning in the forest
Of damp green and nectarous dew

And I woke up thinking I still slept
I still wonder who you are
I'm haunted by the image of
Your crystal eyes and velvet hall

Canicas

La singular condición en que a menudo me
encuentro,
Una que implica un fatal compromiso
Donde mis sueños, canicas (como amuletos)
Se riegan por todo el piso

Si supieras que en tal situación he llorado,
Pensando en que alguna se me haya
perdido
Y si alguien me ayuda, es un caso muy raro
No ocurre ni en cada quince solsticios

De verano, de esos, quince he vivido
(Y no son los veranos que estimo)
Sino las noches de invierno estrelladas, el
cielo
Que capturo en mis negras esferas de vidrio

Si se te riegan los sueños, no pidas ayuda,
Yo sé bien ya por experiencia
Que en canicas con tanto valor lo que ven
No es belleza ni amor, es blasfemia

Mi única joya, mi preciado tesoro
Son mis sueños, canicas - les han dicho feas
Cada vez que se riegan me asusto y yo lloro,
Las recojo antes que alguien me vea

Mirrorglass

Broken mirror glass all over
All over my bedroom floor
Thinking about you and four o clock clouds
Thinking about before

I miss you so, I think and feel
I'd only have you if I drown
The sky is the water, believe it,
That's where everything lost is found

In the sequins of mirrors
The mirrors that flood
My room and remind I miss you so
If I walk on them they will be
Stained red with blood
So I won't move, I have nowhere to go

Motherboard

Fireflies that flutter by
Gentle green light specks, a visual
humming
For lazy eyesight, tiny limelights
One can question what has been and what's
becoming

Insects often imitate
Technology, machines are insect-like -
Spiders made of wires,
Setting small, clear crystal fires
Misfiring, firing, fire, and they strike.

A neuron like a circuit
Is a spiderlight, webs cable like,
They crawl inside your ears, you know,
And set off such annoying lights!

Is it crickets that I hear?
Creak-cricketing in my thoughts?
I'm sorry, I did not hear you,
I think,
CLICK CLICK!
Excuse me, what?

59

Machine

Lifeless, yet moving
cables and rust
diodes and microchips
- an object of lust -

Superior in form
advanced evolution
binary thought patterns
beyond human delusions

Cold glass and metal,
sharp edges, wires
like robot-dreamed up fiction,
the synthflesh of desire

From a vial of glowing fluid
echoes a steady, steady hum
pulsing electronic soundwaves
like a heartbeat, beating, numb

Although it can be taken apart,
although you can make your hands bleed
the memory survives in the wires, the black
blood of the heart of the monster machine

CountDown

10

It starts at dusk, it hits at twelve
Seven hours deep
Into the night, into the dark
When one should be asleep

9

A song, a melody, forgotten
Will play and play and play
And play, but not be reproduced
Just haunt the in-between for days

8

Then thoughts - as words, as images
That shudder in rhythm, deep, like bones
Resound and crash against the skull
Repeating, repeating "you're here, and
alone"

7

Flesh, a prison, flesh, a home...
Confinement, four gray walls
Illusions of flight floating high in the clouds
As you wait for the weight and the fall

6

Then the confusion, then the fear:
A moth bound in a spider's web
What is fiction, what is real?
How to hollow out your head?

5

How to escape the noise, the shaking,
When your heart beats loud and fast?
With sweating, weak and wobbling hands
Unable to do even regular tasks

4

But hands can always hold an object
Close enough to sear the skin
But not to bleed the demons out,
Just mark the body they dwell in

3

Hot tears that sting like alcohol
Making cheeks and temples wet
When lying on a cursed life-bed
Haunted, and desperate and thinking of
death

2

As a child that sucks his thumb
And bites it until it bleeds
Bites until it feels, until
There's nothing more to need

1

Until the day breaks, noise, and noise
And noise, until the day will end
Then night falls with her soft, dark veil
And it begins again, again

Walls

The walls, they whisper things, they say,
They say "you're going to drown
For there are rainclouds near above"
A deluge will pour down

And wash away the ash, but yet,
Create a dirty, gray torrent

Within these four gray walls they will
Sing me a lullaby
Of something mapped out in the stars long
ago,
Something reality could defy

Windowsill

I saw a reflection
In a windowsill
As the rain outside
Stood the moment still

> Awful dreams
> Of bones and dust
> Of metal and glass
> And morbid lust

Diluted, diffused
By drops of rain -
They had clouded the glass,
Made the world outside gray

> But the world was still gray
> When I stepped outside
> I got all wet
> (It was better inside)

Then I looked to the window
And again, saw my face
In the glass, my wet hair
An aesthetic disgrace

> Behind me I saw
> The monsters, all there
> But they're only reflections
> With blunt teeth to bear

You Wouldn't Know

The last time you saw what a morning
looked like
You said you'd dreamed of me
The sky was blue instead of black
And there were smaller things to see

Like little green demons skipping in
puddles
Like flowers that crawled up the fences
Like the tears that fell from invisible angels
And an ill, pallid faith at another's expenses

But you wouldn't know what a morning
looks like
You'd have no remembrance of me,
Of the sky with the clouds and the sunlit
bands,
Or the church-ceiling heavens, you never
did see

Buckled pink shoes with small, colored
hearts,
White hats, flowered ribbons, in blue

Stories of fig trees and houses and pigs
And a ladder to heaven I knew that I knew

The world has gotten bigger, so now
Sleep has become the one god I adore
Sleeping through days, through mornings
and nights
Through life –and ask not why I mourn.

III. In Wilderness

74

Weedsong

I was a weed in a meadow that blossomed
A flower so pretty that butterflies wept
And my beauty, so simple, and yellow and
blue,
As I shone in the sunlight, modest, yet
confident

But showers and winds brought so many
new things
Rosebushes, thornbushes, berries and trees
Tall ones and small ones, not ugly at all
ones,
A forest there grew, and it grew around me

Now, I am pale and weak, and I die as I
speak,
For the sun shines hot through all the
branches up high
But I speak yet, the butterflies hold
memories
Of the meadow with grasses and flowers
like me

Cloudspeak

Silver moonbathed flora
Speaks the hush of the whispering winds
Yet a rumble from under
The ground's muffled thunder
Reveals dormant sickness within

The Cancer will feed and will eat us away
And we'll die in the bile that she spews
The Earth, the raped mother
We have no choice other
Than to find her last gifts to devour and use

Maria

There is a kingdom in the skies, there is
A cathedral home in the air
Where there lives a young queen, a virginal
nymph
With water-like eyes and gold, glowing hair

She's the mother of motherless children,
And hope
You'll return to her arms when you die
Only if you're let in,
 free of all so-called sin,
Back home, to the Cathedral in the Sky

Summer

There's stars inside my eyes, you know
(As fiction, yes, I've told some lies)
But this is true, I'm telling you,
There's stars inside my eyes.

The crystal plasma of liquid space
Is quickly interrupted
By dots of white and specks of light
Like fireflies, minimized

I have been blind at times, I have
And half-blind, less severe
And I have stars inside my eyes
That flash – I've lights instead of tears

Siren

How disturbing is the light in dreams
And visions of a drowning
When one cannot sleep, reason fails
It's the angels, surely frowning

You bring many dreams, deceased, ashore
Like the waves that serve the oceans, deep
(I lament, I grew from child to stone)
They crash against Time's coral reefs

I am a wretched siren, spoiled
You and I both fool what heart I have
I love you, swim these depths with me,
Add pieces to my past...

I'll sing for you, I'll give pure and true
My love 'til forever falls down
Here, underwater, where passions condense
Love eternal, before you have drowned

Your splendid eyes sparkle as light
shimmers through
The green and blue crystalline sea

I shall keep you forever to look at your eyes,
If you wish to stay down here with me

I wish you would, I have seen you in
dreams
But you know, this won't keep me content
To lure you and keep you, my fickle caprice
Until all of my poems are spent

I cannot bear to see you leave
I will cry at seeing you gone
But what of the heavy, dark waters above…
You will drown like remembered and
forgotten songs

Come and go, as does the tide
Commanded by the pale faced moon
Forget me and you'll save your life
But I promise, I would have loved you

Poof!

You'll never know, you'll never know
I flew through the water and danced in the
air
I looked in your eyes, and mine blew you a
kiss,
Then I whisp-walked away with bugs in my
hair

You never touched me, I am like fire
I never saw you,
just looked straight on through

You never saw me, I am the wind,

And like dust blows away,
And stars fade by day

None of this is for you.

Crash

Quisiera ver cada estrella
estrellar como cantos de hielo
delante de mí, contra el piso
y romperse contra el concreto

Y que sea una noche sin luna
para no verme arrodillada
en una noche tan oscura
llorando borbotones de escarcha

Que brillen pequeños fragmentos
como si fueran un gran espejo
que restrayó la fuerza del tiempo
cansado, dolido y eterno

Y que sea tan oscuro que no pueda ver
más que cristales, el hielo y negrura
Con la caricia del aire me basta y me basta
ver estrellas cayendo en las noches sin luna

Love Poem

Forever, stars burn quiet and
the earth breathes slow beneath the sky...
there are no answers anymore
for those who must ask why

Just the sounds of night alone,
the subtle rustling of the leaves
and dreams of that which never was,
floating on the breeze...

I know every single star,
and every star has seen my tears
that fall for every passing day,
as hours turn to years

Your voice rings in my head, the stars
are like the freckles on your skin,
they sparkle like your eyes of light,
but I can't quite remember them...

Every day and every night,
I look out into the sky or sea
and think of you and where you are,
out far beyond what I can see

So I close my eyes and your smile returns
clear,
and you flow through my blood, though
oceans apart
No one so close and no one so dear,
(as the better half of my heart)

I dream with eyes closed for as long as I
can,
and everything changes when opening
them...
 I forget to remember, caught up in the
world,
it all becomes empty and senseless again.

Blue

Why, there was a beach in the sky (or
in/versely)
But both were contained in a song
With a power that's haunted me, worsely,
I've been hearing it for so long…

Since that day on the oceanside,
Where I met a girl, her name was Blue
She lived there, at the ocean's side
With nothing in the world to do

So I asked this girl, the blue haired blue,
"What do you do each day?"
And she replied, "I watch the skies,
And listen to the glittering waves."

Still, I wondered where she lived,
At night, where did she sleep?
She said "I live where I am standing
And I dream in yonder coral reefs."

"Do you tire of the sand and sun,
Or living like no human could?"
"My dear, I am not human,
You may not understand, no human could."

Mystified I was by she,
of pale skin and crystal eyes
She danced at the shore, commanding the waves
And plainly seducing the skies.

I felt envy's teeth as the ripped at my neck
For she was a child of the sun
That made me realize to the truth I'm confined
That I'm as enslaved as they come

She danced and she twirled, unclothed except
for
Some bracelets and anklets and blue-green glass
beads
To match her matted cobalt hair
And her eyes of the brightest emerald green

To the shore where she gracefully frolicked
I walked to her, with my black parasol
"Blue, do you tire of being by yourself,
Do you ever get lonely at all?"

She frowned for a moment, shrugged and then
grinned,
She answered an honest "Nope.
I rebelled against Time, and I'm fine, I am fine,
I am lulled by the sea's serenade.
I will never age, I will never feel change,

But at dusk and at dawn, with the shifting of
rays."
So I nodded and held my hand up to her cheek
And turned from her to travel back where I
belong
But she gave me a bracelet made out of glass
beads,
And as I walked away, she sang a sweet song.

And I, as death's kin do not dream, yet I wish
That I could forget Blue, the Neptunian nymph,

And the sky in water, the beach in the sky,
The sky I thought mine until I saw it claimed
By the Ocean's blue daughter, ever young,
bright and blue,
That His will always remain.

Papersnake

"Yes, I want to be like you,"
said the girl to the amber-leaf tree.

A spiral,
a white ribbon
slithered about in the air
with a most curious,
dry,
paper sound.

The girl reached out and took the ribbon,
upon which was written:

IT IS TIME FOR YOU TO COMB AWAY
THOSE STARS THAT FELL ONTO YOUR
HAIR.

"Stars?" she thought, "I've no stars in my
hair."

So she let the ribbon go
and the ribbon slithered off.
When she looked up at the tree,
at its amber leaves,

she smiled.

She kissed its trunk, standing on her toes,
as high as she could reach,
and skipped away.

Papersky

The voice that writes I do not recognize,
I do not think…
Well, each poem has a voice that's all its
own
There's rust in this one…

The time has come

To retire

From the wires

And come home.